# Alphabet Fun

## Making Letters With Your Body

Isabel Thomas

**Heinemann** LIBRARY

Chicago, Illinois

To contact Capstone Global Library please phone 800-747-4992, or
visit our website www.capstonepub.com

Edited by Dan Nunn and Helen Cox Cannons
Designed by Tim Bond
Original illustrations © Capstone Global Library, Ltd, 2014
Picture research by Elizabeth Alexander
Production by Helen McCreath
Originated by Capstone Global Library, Ltd
Printed and bound in China by Leo Paper Products, Ltd

21 20 19 18 17
10 9 8 7 6 5 4 3 2

**Library of Congress Cataloging-in-Publication Data**
Thomas, Isabel, 1980-
  Alphabet fun : making letters with your body / Isabel Thomas.
    pages cm
  Includes bibliographical references.
  ISBN 978-1-4329-8802-9 (hb)—ISBN 978-1-4329-8803-6 (pb)  1. English
language—Alphabet—Juvenile literature. 2. Alphabet books—
Juvenile literature. 3. Movement education. 4. Motor learning.  I. Title.
  PE1155.T64 2014
   421'.1—dc23                    2013019894

**Acknowledgments**
The author and publisher are grateful to the following for permission
to reproduce copyright material: all body letters A–Z, on all pages
© Capstone Publishers (Karon Dubke); balls in letters I and J,
Shutterstock (© Eric Milos, © Feng Yu).

Cover photograph of body letters reproduced with permission of
© Capstone Publishers (Karon Dubke).

The author would like to thank Polly Barker, Archie Catterall, Edward
Cullum, Ethan Parsons, Eliza Redding, Harry Sample, and Joey
Sample for their invaluable help in the preparation of this book.

# Getting Started

Do these things as you look through the book:

- Name the letters of the alphabet.

- Make the letter sounds.

- Find letters made from straight lines.

- Find letters made from curvy lines.

- Find letters made from straight and curvy lines.

- Name the parts of the body that you see. The list on the glossary page will help you.

- Make letter shapes with your body.

Aa

# Bb

Cc

Dd

Ee

Ff

Gg

Hh

Ii

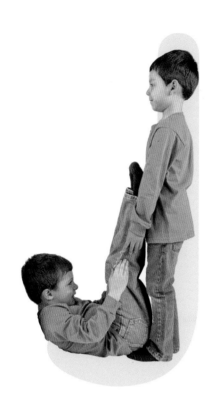

Jj

Kk

Ll

Mm

# Nn

Oo

Pp

Qq

Rr

Ss

T t

Uu

Vv

Ww

# Xx

Yy

Zz

# Activities

## Can you make body letters?

- Make uppercase letters by stretching up high.

- Make lowercase letters by curling up tight.

- Make letter shapes standing up, sitting down, and lying on the floor.

- Work with a friend to make body letters with two people.

## Activities for pairs and groups

- Work as a team to spell simple words or names.

- Play body letter charades. One pair or team makes a letter shape. Another pair or team has to guess which letter they are making.

- Practice giving instructions. Tell others how to make a mystery letter by telling them which shapes to make with their body. Take a digital photograph (or play in front of a large mirror). Ask them to guess which letter they have made.

- Make a class alphabet. Take photographs of children making each body letter in front of a white background. You could use a computer to turn the photographs into silhouettes.

- Play musical letters. Dance until the music stops, then make the letter shape that is held up or called out.

# My Body: Picture Glossary

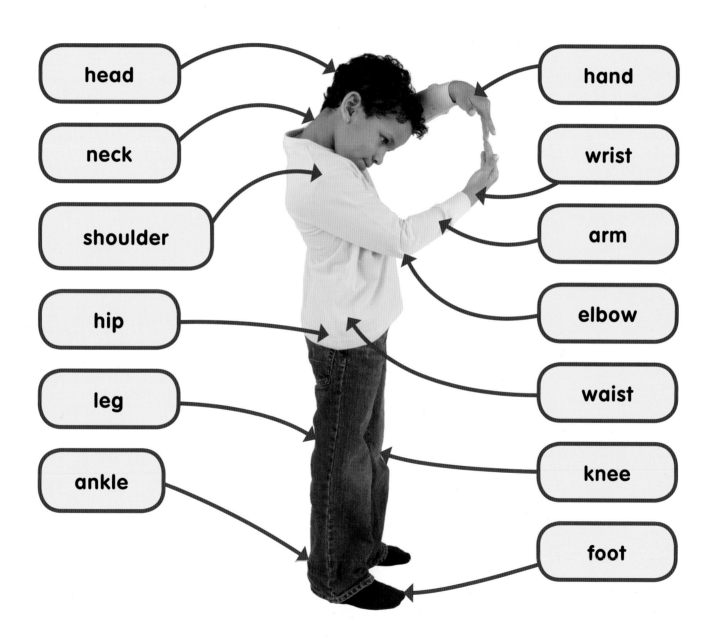

head

neck

shoulder

hip

leg

ankle

hand

wrist

arm

elbow

waist

knee

foot

# Notes for Parents and Teachers

There are lots of different ways to use *Alphabet Fun*. Beginning readers will enjoy looking at the photographs and talking about how each letter is formed. Use the information in the introduction to explore the book together.

Active learners will enjoy making letter shapes by using their own body. They can use the ideas in the book, or find new ways to make each letter. Take photographs and compare them to the pictures in the book. Which letter shapes were easiest to make and why?

The activities on the previous page are ideas for combining literacy learning and physical development. The games encourage children to use letter names, movement words, and the names of body parts. Practice forming body letters in pairs or in groups. Try moving at different speeds and holding each shape to help children develop balance and coordination.